INDOOR GARDENING
FOR BEGINNERS

SHANA KEITH

TABLE OF CONTENT

GARDEN PLANNER

GARDEN PLANNER

Common Name:	Botanical Name:
Crop Variety:	Date Planted:
Date Harvested:	Date Transplanted:

☐ Flower ☐ Fruit ☐ Herb ☐ Vegetable ☐ Tree

☐ Annual	☐ Edible	☐ Medicinal
☐ Perennial	☐ Spices	☐ Repellent
☐ Biennial	☐ Tea	☐ Natural Dyes

Purchased Information:	Watering Schedule:
Vendor:	
Cost:	Sunlight Exposure:
Quantity Purchased:	
Care Instructions:	Disease/Insects Problems:
	Treatments and Results:
Fertilizers to Use:	Additional Notes:

INTRODUCTION

Welcome to the world of indoor gardening, where the beauty of nature meets the comforts of your home.

This beginner's guide is your key to cultivating a thriving oasis of greenery within the confines of your living space. Indoor gardening is not just about adding aesthetic appeal; it's a journey that reconnects you with nature, reduces stress, and introduces you to the joy of nurturing life.

In the chapters that follow, we will embark on a comprehensive exploration of the fundamental principles of indoor gardening.

From selecting the right plants and creating an ideal environment to mastering the art of watering and nutrient management, this guide is designed to empower beginners with the knowledge needed to foster a flourishing indoor garden.

Discover the joy of transforming your home into a vibrant sanctuary where plants thrive and contribute to your well-being.

Whether you're a complete novice or have dabbled in gardening before, this guide is your compass in navigating the fascinating realm of indoor gardening. So, let's embark on this green journey together and unlock the secrets to cultivating a lush, thriving indoor garden that not only enhances your living space but also enriches your life.

GARDEN PLANNER

GARDEN PLANNER

Common Name:	Botanical Name:
Crop Variety:	Date Planted:
Date Harvested:	Date Transplanted:

☐ Flower ☐ Fruit ☐ Herb ☐ Vegetable ☐ Tree

☐ Annual   ☐ Edible   ☐ Medicinal

☐ Perennial   ☐ Spices   ☐ Repellent

☐ Biennial   ☐ Tea   ☐ Natural Dyes

Purchased Information:	Watering Schedule:
Vendor:	
Cost:	Sunlight Exposure:
Quantity Purchased:	
Care Instructions:	Disease/Insects Problems:
	Treatments and Results:
Fertilizers to Use:	Additional Notes:

GARDEN PLANNER

GARDEN PLANNER

Common Name:	Botanical Name:
Crop Variety:	Date Planted:
Date Harvested:	Date Transplanted:

☐ Flower   ☐ Fruit   ☐ Herb   ☐ Vegetable   ☐ Tree

☐ Annual   ☐ Edible   ☐ Medicinal

☐ Perennial   ☐ Spices   ☐ Repellent

☐ Biennial   ☐ Tea   ☐ Natural Dyes

Purchased Information:

Watering Schedule:

Vendor:

Cost:

Sunlight Exposure:

Quantity Purchased:

Care Instructions:

Disease/Insects Problems:

Treatments and Results:

Fertilizers to Use:

Additional Notes:

CHAPTER ONE:

GETTING STARTED

Introduction to Indoor Gardening

Indoor gardening is a captivating endeavor that brings the wonders of nature into the heart of your home. Unlike traditional outdoor gardening, indoor gardening allows you to create a lush and thriving ecosystem within the controlled environment of your living space. This practice has gained immense popularity, offering a unique blend of aesthetics, mental well-being, and the joy of nurturing living organisms. The primary allure of indoor gardening lies in its accessibility to individuals with limited outdoor space or adverse weather conditions. It transforms any room into a haven of greenery, where plants not only add visual appeal but also contribute to the overall ambiance. Whether you're a gardening enthusiast or a novice with no prior experience, the indoor gardening journey begins with a sense of curiosity and a desire to cultivate life within the confines of your home.

In this introduction, we'll explore the fundamental aspects of indoor gardening. From the selection of suitable plants to understanding the key environmental factors, every step plays a crucial role in the success of your indoor garden. As we delve deeper into the subsequent chapters, you'll discover the joy of hands-on cultivation, gain insights into plant care, and unravel the therapeutic benefits of fostering a green sanctuary within your own living space. Get ready to embark on a rewarding journey where nature and nurture come together in the art of indoor gardening.

Benefits of Indoor Gardening

Indoor gardening extends far beyond the aesthetic appeal of having verdant foliage within your living space; it encompasses a spectrum of physical, mental, and environmental advantages.

1. Enhanced Air Quality:

Indoor plants act as natural air purifiers, absorbing pollutants and releasing oxygen. They can mitigate the impact of indoor air pollutants, such as volatile organic compounds (VOCs), providing a healthier breathing environment.

2. Stress Reduction:

The presence of greenery has been linked to stress reduction and improved mental well-being. Indoor gardening offers a therapeutic escape, fostering a calming atmosphere that can alleviate anxiety and enhance overall mood.

3. Connection with Nature:

Indoor gardening allows individuals to establish a profound connection with nature, even in urban or confined living spaces. Caring for plants provides a sense of purpose and nurtures a deeper appreciation for the natural world.

4. Improved Focus and Productivity:

Studies suggest that the introduction of indoor plants in work or study spaces can enhance concentration and productivity. The visual appeal of plants and the oxygen they release contribute to a more conducive environment for cognitive tasks.

5. Temperature and Humidity Regulation:

Plants naturally release moisture through a process called transpiration. This not only helps regulate indoor humidity levels but also contributes to a more comfortable and balanced temperature in your living environment.

6. Decorative Appeal:

Beyond their health benefits, indoor plants serve as elegant and versatile decor elements. They bring vibrancy, texture, and color to indoor spaces, enhancing the overall visual appeal of your home.

7. Edible Harvests:

Some indoor gardens focus on growing edible plants, providing a fresh and sustainable source of herbs, vegetables, or fruits. This not only supports a healthier diet but also fosters a sense of accomplishment.

8. Year-Round Gardening:

Unlike outdoor gardening, indoor gardening allows you to cultivate plants year-round, irrespective of weather conditions. This continuity provides a consistent source of joy and engagement.

Understanding and embracing these multifaceted benefits of indoor gardening not only enhances the quality of your living space but also contributes to a holistic and balanced lifestyle. Whether you are an urban dweller or a gardening enthusiast, the rewards of cultivating an indoor garden extend far beyond the boundaries of your potted plants.

Selecting the Right Plants for Indoors:

Choosing the appropriate plants is a crucial step in creating a successful indoor garden. Factors such as light conditions, available space, and individual preferences play pivotal roles in determining which plants will thrive within the confines of your home.

1. Light Requirements:

Assess the natural light available in your indoor space. Different plants have varying light preferences—some thrive in bright, direct sunlight, while others flourish in low-light conditions. Consider the orientation of windows and the intensity and duration of sunlight exposure when choosing your plants.

2. Space Constraints:

Take into account the available space in your home. Compact or trailing plants might be suitable for smaller spaces, while larger rooms can accommodate taller or bushier varieties. Vertical gardening solutions or hanging planters can also maximize space utilization.

3. Temperature Tolerance:

Consider the temperature range within your home. Some plants are more sensitive to temperature fluctuations, while others are adaptable to a broader range. Understanding the temperature requirements of your chosen plants is essential for their overall health and vitality.

4. Humidity Preferences:

Indoor environments can vary in humidity levels. Certain plants, such as tropical varieties, thrive in higher humidity, while others, like succulents, prefer drier conditions. Match the humidity preferences of your chosen plants with the ambient conditions of your home.

5. Maintenance and Care:

Assess your commitment to plant care. Some plants are more forgiving and resilient, requiring minimal attention, while others may demand more meticulous care. Choose plants that align with your schedule and level of experience, ensuring a positive and sustainable gardening experience.

6. Allergies and Pet-Friendly Varieties:

Consider any allergies or pets in your home. Some plants may trigger allergic reactions, while others can be toxic to pets. Opt for non-toxic and allergy-friendly plants to create a safe and harmonious environment for everyone in your household.

7. Aesthetic Preferences:

Reflect on the aesthetic you want to achieve. Whether you prefer lush greenery, colorful blooms, or architectural foliage, there's a vast array of indoor plants to suit your taste. Mixing and matching different plant varieties can create visually appealing and dynamic indoor landscapes.

8. Purpose of Gardening:

Define the purpose of your indoor garden. Are you cultivating plants for decoration, air purification, or even for edible harvests? Align your plant selections with your gardening goals to ensure a fulfilling and purposeful experience.

By carefully considering these factors, you can curate an indoor garden that not only survives but thrives in your unique living environment. The right selection of plants sets the foundation for a rewarding and enjoyable indoor gardening journey.

Essential Tools and Supplies for Indoor Gardening

Embarking on a successful indoor gardening journey requires a set of essential tools and supplies to ensure that you can nurture and care for your plants effectively.

1. Containers and Pots:

Select appropriate containers based on the size and type of plants you're cultivating. Ensure that containers have drainage holes to prevent waterlogged soil, promoting optimal root health. Consider the material of the pots, such as ceramic, plastic, or fabric, based on your aesthetic preferences and practical needs.

2. Potting Mix:

Choose a high-quality potting mix suitable for indoor plants. These mixes provide a well-balanced combination of nutrients, aeration, and drainage. Avoid using garden soil, as it may compact over time and hinder plant growth.

3. Watering Can or Sprayer:

A watering can with a narrow spout or a spray bottle is essential for precise watering, especially in smaller indoor spaces. This allows you to control water distribution and avoid over-saturation.

4. Pruning Shears or Scissors:

Pruning shears or scissors are indispensable for maintaining the health and shape of your indoor plants. Regular pruning helps remove dead or yellowing leaves, encourages bushier growth, and prevents the spread of diseases.

5. Hand Trowel or Small Shovel:

For transplanting or adding soil to pots, a hand trowel or small shovel is invaluable. Choose one with a comfortable grip for ease of use in confined spaces.

6. Gloves:

Protect your hands from soil, moisture, and potential irritants by wearing gardening gloves. Look for breathable and flexible options to ensure comfort during extended gardening sessions.

7. Indoor Plant Fertilizer:

Indoor plants benefit from regular feeding. Choose a balanced indoor plant fertilizer or a specific formulation based on the needs of your plants. Follow recommended application rates to avoid over-fertilization.

8. pH Testing Kit:

Monitoring the pH level of your potting mix is crucial for plant health. A pH testing kit helps you adjust the acidity or alkalinity of the soil, ensuring optimal nutrient absorption by your plants.

9. Humidity Tray:

A humidity tray filled with water and pebbles placed beneath your plants helps increase ambient humidity, especially in drier indoor environments. This is particularly beneficial for plants with higher humidity requirements.

10.   Plant Labels:

Keep track of your plant varieties by using plant labels. This simple tool helps you remember specific care instructions, watering schedules, and the names of your beloved indoor greenery.

11. Grow Lights:

Supplemental lighting becomes essential in spaces with limited natural light. Choose LED grow lights that provide the right spectrum for plant growth. Position lights at the correct distance from your plants to avoid issues like stretching or scorching.

Having these essential tools and supplies on hand will empower you to create and maintain a flourishing indoor garden, ensuring that your plants receive the care and attention they deserve.

Planning Your Indoor Garden Space:

Designing an indoor garden space requires thoughtful consideration to maximize the potential for plant growth and create an aesthetically pleasing environment within the confines of your home.

1. Evaluate Light Conditions:

Identify the natural light sources in your home, such as windows or skylights. Different plants have varying light requirements, so assess the intensity and duration of sunlight exposure in different areas. Place light-loving plants closer to windows, while low-light varieties can thrive in more shaded spots.

2. Understand Microclimates:

Indoor spaces can have microclimates influenced by factors like temperature, humidity, and airflow. Analyze these microclimates to determine suitable plant placements. For example, avoid placing heat-sensitive plants near radiators or drafty areas.

3. Optimize Space Utilization:

Make the most of your available space by utilizing vertical gardening solutions, hanging planters, or shelving units. This not only maximizes the number of plants you can accommodate but also adds visual interest to your indoor garden.

4. Consider Plant Sizes and Growth Habits:

Take into account the eventual size and growth habits of your chosen plants. Ensure that taller plants are positioned at the back or center of the garden, while shorter or trailing varieties can be placed towards the front or edges.

5. Group Plants with Similar Needs:

Cluster plants with similar light, humidity, and watering requirements together. This simplifies care routines, allowing you to provide consistent conditions for grouped plants and avoid potential conflicts in their care.

6. Create Design Focal Points:

Intentionally arrange plants to create focal points within your indoor garden. Consider placing a statement plant or a group of visually striking varieties to enhance the overall aesthetic appeal of the space.

7. Provide Adequate Airflow:

Ensure proper ventilation within your indoor garden to prevent stagnant air, which can lead to issues like mold or pest infestations. Positioning plants with some space between them facilitates airflow and promotes a healthier growing environment.

8. Account for Accessibility:

Plan for easy access to your plants for routine care and maintenance. Avoid placing plants in hard-to-reach areas, making it convenient for watering, pruning, and inspecting your green companions.

Incorporate Decorative Elements:

Enhance the visual appeal of your indoor garden by incorporating decorative elements such as stylish planters, decorative pots, or complementary accessories. Consider the overall aesthetic you want to achieve to create a cohesive and pleasing design.

9. Adaptability and Flexibility:

Recognize that the needs of your indoor garden may change over time. Choose furniture and containers that are easy to move, allowing you to adapt the layout as your plant collection evolves or as seasons change.

By carefully planning your indoor garden space, you can create a harmonious and thriving oasis that complements your living environment. Thoughtful consideration of light, space, and aesthetics ensures a rewarding and enjoyable indoor gardening experience.

GARDEN PLANNER

GARDEN PLANNER

Common Name:	Botanical Name:
Crop Variety:	Date Planted:
Date Harvested:	Date Transplanted:

☐ Flower ☐ Fruit ☐ Herb ☐ Vegetable ☐ Tree

☐ Annual	☐ Edible	☐ Medicinal
☐ Perennial	☐ Spices	☐ Repellent
☐ Biennial	☐ Tea	☐ Natural Dyes

Purchased Information:	Watering Schedule:
Vendor:	
Cost:	Sunlight Exposure:
Quantity Purchased:	
Care Instructions:	Disease/Insects Problems:
	Treatments and Results:
Fertilizers to Use:	Additional Notes:

GARDEN PLANNER

GARDEN PLANNER

Common Name:	Botanical Name:
Crop Variety:	Date Planted:
Date Harvested:	Date Transplanted:

☐ Flower ☐ Fruit ☐ Herb ☐ Vegetable ☐ Tree

☐ Annual	☐ Edible	☐ Medicinal
☐ Perennial	☐ Spices	☐ Repellent
☐ Biennial	☐ Tea	☐ Natural Dyes

Purchased Information:

Vendor:

Cost:

Quantity Purchased:

Watering Schedule:

Sunlight Exposure:

Care Instructions:

Fertilizers to Use:

Disease/Insects Problems:

Treatments and Results:

Additional Notes:

CHAPTER TWO:

SETTING UP YOUR INDOOR GARDEN

Choosing the Right Containers

Selecting the appropriate containers for your indoor plants is a critical aspect of ensuring their health and promoting successful growth. Consider the following factors when choosing containers for your indoor garden:

1. Size Matters:

Choose containers that provide ample space for the roots to grow. Larger plants generally require larger pots to prevent them from becoming root-bound. Conversely, smaller plants may struggle in oversized containers, as excess soil retains more moisture.

2. Drainage Holes:

Opt for containers with drainage holes to prevent waterlogging and ensure proper aeration of the soil. Excess water drainage is crucial for preventing root rot and other water-related issues.

3. Material Selection:

Containers come in various materials, each with its own advantages. Terracotta and clay pots are porous and allow for good airflow, but they dry out faster. Plastic containers are lightweight and retain moisture well. Choose the material that best suits the needs of your specific plants and the conditions in your home.

4. Weight Considerations:

Take into account the weight of the containers, especially if you plan to move them frequently or if your indoor space has weight restrictions. Lightweight materials like plastic or fiberglass may be more suitable for larger plants.

5. Aesthetic Appeal:

Consider the aesthetic impact of the containers within your indoor space. Coordinated or complementary colors and styles can enhance the overall visual appeal of your indoor garden. Experiment with different shapes and textures to create a diverse and interesting display.

6. Self-Watering Options:

For individuals with busy schedules or those who may forget to water regularly, self-watering containers can be a practical solution. These containers have built-in reservoirs that supply water to the soil as needed, reducing the risk of over or under-watering.

7. Ease of Cleaning:

Indoor containers may accumulate dust or mineral deposits over time. Choose containers that are easy to clean, ensuring a tidy and healthy environment for your plants.

8. Temperature Considerations:

Some materials, like metal or dark-colored pots, can absorb and retain heat. In warmer climates or near sources of direct sunlight, consider lighter-colored containers to prevent the soil from overheating.

9. Versatility:

Consider the versatility of the containers. Some plants may benefit from being moved outdoors during favorable weather conditions. Choose containers that are easy to transport and adapt to different environments.

10.   Saucers or Trays:

Place containers on saucers or trays to catch excess water and prevent damage to surfaces. This not only helps in maintaining cleanliness but also provides a visual uniformity to your indoor garden.

11. Consider Plant Specifics:

Tailor your container choices to the specific needs of your plants. For example, shallow-rooted plants may thrive in wider containers, while deep-rooted plants benefit from deeper pots.

By carefully selecting containers based on these considerations, you can create an optimal environment for your indoor plants, ensuring their well-being and contributing to the overall success of your indoor gardening endeavors.

Selecting the Ideal Potting Mix for Indoor Gardening

Choosing the right potting mix is crucial for the health and vitality of your indoor plants. A well-balanced mix provides essential nutrients, proper aeration, and optimal water retention. Consider the following factors when selecting the ideal potting mix for your indoor garden:

1. Container Type:

Different containers and plants have varied moisture retention capabilities. Tailor your potting mix to suit the specific needs of your plants and the type of containers you are using. Ensure good drainage for containers with drainage holes.

2. Soil Structure:

Opt for a potting mix with a light and airy structure to promote healthy root growth. A mix that is too dense can lead to compacted soil, hindering root development and nutrient absorption.

3. Nutrient Content:

Look for a potting mix enriched with essential nutrients. While some mixes contain slow-release fertilizers, others may require additional fertilization. Choose a mix that aligns with the nutrient requirements of your specific plants.

4. pH Levels:

Ensure that the potting mix has a suitable pH level for the plants you are cultivating. Most indoor plants prefer a slightly acidic to neutral pH. Adjustments can be made using additives or amendments if necessary.

5. Water Retention:

Balancing water retention is crucial. The potting mix should hold enough water to keep the soil consistently moist but not waterlogged. Adequate drainage prevents root rot and other water-related issues.

6. Sterilization:

Choose a potting mix that has been sterilized to eliminate pathogens, pests, and weed seeds. Sterilized mixes contribute to a healthier growing environment and reduce the risk of plant diseases.

7. Peat or Coco Coir:

Many potting mixes include peat moss or coco coir as organic components. These materials provide water retention and aeration. Consider your sustainability preferences and the environmental impact of the materials used in the mix.

8. Perlite or Vermiculite:

These materials enhance aeration and drainage in potting mixes. Perlite is lightweight and prevents compaction, while vermiculite retains moisture. Their inclusion contributes to a well-balanced and fluffy potting mix.

9. Compost or Organic Matter:

Incorporating compost or well-rotted organic matter enriches the potting mix with nutrients. Organic matter also improves soil structure and provides a beneficial environment for beneficial microorganisms.

10.   Specialty Mixes for Specific Plants:

Some plants, such as orchids or succulents, have unique growing requirements. Consider specialty potting mixes tailored to the needs of specific plant types to ensure optimal growing conditions.

11. Brand and Quality:

Choose potting mixes from reputable brands known for their quality. High-quality mixes may cost a bit more, but they often result in healthier and more vigorous plants.

12. Moisture-Conserving Additives:

Some potting mixes include moisture-conserving additives like water-absorbing crystals. These can be beneficial for those who may not have consistent watering schedules.

By considering these factors, you can select a potting mix that provides the essential elements for your indoor plants, creating an environment conducive to healthy growth and vibrant foliage.

Understanding Light Requirements for Indoor Plants

Proper light is a fundamental factor in the health and growth of indoor plants. Different plants have varying light requirements, and understanding these needs is crucial for creating an optimal environment.

1. Light Intensity:

Different plants thrive in different light intensities. Assess the natural light available in your indoor space and categorize it into low, medium, or bright light conditions. This classification helps in selecting plants that match the light levels in specific areas of your home.

2. Duration of Light Exposure:

Consider the duration of light exposure your plants receive. Some plants prefer longer periods of bright light, while others can tolerate lower light levels. Understand the daily light cycle in your home and position plants accordingly.

3. Direct vs. Indirect Light:

Identify whether your indoor space provides direct sunlight or if light is filtered through curtains or windows. Some plants, like succulents, may thrive in direct sunlight, while others, such as ferns, prefer indirect or filtered light.

4. North, South, East, or West-Facing Windows:

The orientation of windows affects the quality and intensity of light. North-facing windows generally receive lower light levels, while south-facing windows receive more direct sunlight. Plants with high light requirements are better suited to south or west-facing windows.

5. Light Measurement:

Consider using a light meter to quantify the light levels in different areas of your home. This tool can help you identify spots with optimal light for specific plant species.

6. Adaptability of Plants:

Some plants are more adaptable to varying light conditions. Pothos, snake plants, and ZZ plants, for example, are known for their ability to thrive in low-light environments. Understanding the adaptability of your chosen plants allows for better placement.

7. Supplemental Lighting:

In spaces with limited natural light, consider incorporating supplemental lighting. LED grow lights are an excellent option for providing the necessary spectrum of light for plant growth. Position lights at the correct distance to avoid issues like leggy growth or leaf burn.

8. Seasonal Adjustments:

Be aware that light conditions may vary with the changing seasons. Adjust the placement of your plants accordingly, especially if they are near windows. Monitor how the angle of the sun changes throughout the year.

9. Light Spectrum:

Plants require specific light spectra for different stages of growth. The full spectrum of light includes blue light for vegetative growth and red light for flowering and fruiting. LED grow lights designed to mimic natural sunlight provide a balanced spectrum for indoor plants.

10.   Leaf Color and Response:

Monitor the color and condition of your plant's leaves. Yellowing or leggy growth may indicate insufficient light, while scorched or browned leaves may suggest too much direct sunlight.

Understanding the light requirements of your indoor plants empowers you to create a well-balanced and thriving environment. By strategically placing plants based on their light preferences, you can enjoy healthy and vibrant greenery in your home.

Temperature and Humidity Considerations for Indoor Gardening

Maintaining the right temperature and humidity levels is essential for the well-being of your indoor plants. Different plant species have specific preferences, and understanding these considerations ensures a conducive environment for growth. Here's a detailed exploration of temperature and humidity factors for successful indoor gardening:

Temperature Considerations:

1. **Ideal Temperature Range:**

Identify the ideal temperature range for your indoor plants. Most common houseplants thrive in temperatures between

60°F to 75°F (15°C to 24°C) during the day and a slightly cooler range at night.

2. Avoid Drastic Temperature Fluctuations:

Aim for stable temperatures and avoid drastic fluctuations. Sudden temperature changes can stress plants and lead to issues like leaf drop or slowed growth.

3. Consider Plant Origin:

Understand the natural habitat of your plants. Some species are native to tropical climates and prefer warmer conditions, while others, like succulents, tolerate lower temperatures.

4. Seasonal Adjustments:

Adjust indoor temperatures seasonally. Many plants benefit from a slight drop in temperature during the winter, simulating their natural dormant period.

5. Protect Plants from Drafts:

Shield plants from drafts, especially cold drafts from windows or doors. Cold drafts can lead to temperature stress and negatively impact plant health.

6. Heating and Cooling Devices:

Use heating or cooling devices as needed to maintain optimal temperatures. Be cautious with space heaters and air conditioners to prevent extreme conditions around your plants.

Humidity Considerations:

1. **Ideal Humidity Levels:**

Determine the ideal humidity levels for your plants. Most indoor plants thrive in a humidity range of 40% to 60%. However, some tropical plants may prefer higher humidity.

2. **Increase Humidity with Methods:**

Increase humidity through methods like misting, using a humidity tray, or grouping plants together. Placing a tray of water filled with pebbles beneath plants helps elevate humidity levels around them.

3. **Monitor Indoor Humidity:**

Regularly monitor indoor humidity levels, especially during the winter when heating systems can reduce moisture in the air. Humidity meters or hygrometers can be useful tools for accurate measurements.

4. **Ventilation and Air Circulation:**

Ensure proper ventilation and air circulation to prevent stagnant air. Good airflow helps regulate humidity and prevents issues like fungal growth.

5. **Avoid Overwatering:**

Be cautious not to overwater your plants, as excessively wet soil can contribute to high humidity levels. Allow the topsoil to dry out slightly between waterings.

6. **Humidity-Loving Plants:**

If you have humidity-loving plants, create microclimates with higher moisture levels by grouping them together or placing them in a bathroom or kitchen where humidity tends to be naturally higher.

7. Dehumidifiers:

In environments with excessively high humidity, consider using dehumidifiers to maintain optimal levels. This is particularly important for preventing mold and mildew growth.

Understanding and managing temperature and humidity considerations contribute to a thriving indoor garden. By tailoring these factors to the specific needs of your plants, you create an environment where they can flourish and remain resilient to potential stressors.

Proper Ventilation for Healthy Plants in Indoor Gardening

Ensuring adequate ventilation is a crucial component of maintaining a healthy indoor garden. Proper airflow not only regulates temperature and humidity but also prevents issues such as mold, fungal diseases, and stagnant air.

1. Air Exchange Rate:

Aim for a regular exchange of air within your indoor space. Opening windows periodically or using fans helps replace stale air with fresh, oxygen-rich air, benefiting both plants and humans.

2. Strategic Placement of Fans:

Position fans strategically to enhance air circulation. Oscillating fans are effective in creating gentle airflow, preventing stagnant pockets of air around plants. Ensure that the fan is not directly blowing on the plants, as excessive wind can lead to moisture loss.

3. Avoid Stagnant Air:

Stagnant air can contribute to issues like mold and mildew. Arrange plants to allow for proper air movement and avoid overcrowding, which can impede airflow.

4. Natural Ventilation:

Take advantage of natural ventilation by opening windows and doors, especially during mild weather. This helps in refreshing the air and regulating temperature and humidity levels.

5. Bathroom and Kitchen Ventilation:

Place plants in or near bathrooms and kitchens where ventilation systems are typically present. These areas often have built-in exhaust fans that aid in maintaining proper air quality.

6. Clean Air Ducts and Filters:

Regularly clean air ducts and filters in heating, ventilation, and air conditioning (HVAC) systems. Clean systems ensure that the air circulated is free from dust and contaminants that could affect both plants and occupants.

7. Monitor Indoor Air Quality:

Invest in indoor air quality monitors to track pollutants and ensure a healthy environment. Addressing indoor air quality issues promptly is vital for the well-being of both plants and individuals.

8. Ventilation during Plant Care:

Provide additional ventilation during activities such as watering, fertilizing, or applying treatments. This helps disperse any fumes or airborne particles that may be released during these processes.

9. Controlled Cross-Ventilation:

Arrange plants to facilitate controlled cross-ventilation. This can be achieved by placing plants near windows or openings on opposite sides of the room, allowing air to flow through the space.

10.   Humidity Control:

Proper ventilation helps control humidity levels. High humidity can contribute to mold growth and other issues. Ensure that the indoor space is well-ventilated to maintain optimal humidity.

11. Isolate Sick Plants:

If a plant shows signs of disease, isolate it from others to prevent the spread of pathogens. Proper ventilation minimizes the risk of diseases spreading through the air.

12. Consideration of Outdoor Conditions:

Be mindful of outdoor air quality and conditions. Avoid keeping windows open during times of high pollution, as this can introduce contaminants to your indoor space.

By incorporating these ventilation strategies, you create a dynamic and healthy environment for your indoor plants. Proper airflow is essential for preventing common issues associated with stagnant air, contributing to the overall well-being and vitality of your indoor garden.

GARDEN PLANNER

GARDEN PLANNER

Common Name:	Botanical Name:
Crop Variety:	Date Planted:
Date Harvested:	Date Transplanted:

☐ Flower ☐ Fruit ☐ Herb ☐ Vegetable ☐ Tree

☐ Annual ☐ Edible ☐ Medicinal

☐ Perennial ☐ Spices ☐ Repellent

☐ Biennial ☐ Tea ☐ Natural Dyes

Purchased Information:	Watering Schedule:
Vendor:	
Cost:	Sunlight Exposure:
Quantity Purchased:	
Care Instructions:	Disease/Insects Problems:
	Treatments and Results:
Fertilizers to Use:	Additional Notes:

GARDEN PLANNER

GARDEN PLANNER

Common Name:	Botanical Name:
Crop Variety:	Date Planted:
Date Harvested:	Date Transplanted:

☐ Flower ☐ Fruit ☐ Herb ☐ Vegetable ☐ Tree

☐ Annual ☐ Edible ☐ Medicinal

☐ Perennial ☐ Spices ☐ Repellent

☐ Biennial ☐ Tea ☐ Natural Dyes

Purchased Information:

Vendor:

Cost:

Quantity Purchased:

Watering Schedule:

Sunlight Exposure:

Care Instructions:

Fertilizers to Use:

Disease/Insects Problems:

Treatments and Results:

Additional Notes:

CHAPTER THREE:

WATERING AND NUTRIENT MANAGEMENT

Watering Basics for Indoor Plants

Watering is a fundamental aspect of caring for indoor plants, and understanding the basics ensures the health and vitality of your green companions.

1. Consistent Moisture:

Maintain consistent moisture levels in the soil. While different plants have varying water requirements, most indoor plants prefer the soil to be evenly moist, not waterlogged or overly dry.

2. Check Soil Moisture:

Regularly check the moisture level of the soil by inserting your finger into the top inch. Water when the soil feels slightly dry. Adjust your watering frequency based on the specific needs of each plant.

3. Water Quality:

Use room temperature water to avoid shocking plant roots. Allow tap water to sit for a day to allow chlorine to dissipate, especially if your plants are sensitive to it. Some plants, like orchids, may benefit from rainwater or distilled water.

4. Bottom Watering:

Consider bottom watering for plants that are sensitive to water on their foliage. Place the pot in a saucer of water and allow the soil to absorb moisture from the bottom. This method prevents the risk of fungal issues on leaves.

5. Avoid Overwatering:

Overwatering is a common issue. Ensure proper drainage in your pots, and allow excess water to escape through drainage holes. Soggy soil can lead to root rot and other moisture-related problems.

6. Understand Plant Watering Needs:

Different plants have different watering needs. Succulents generally require infrequent but deep watering, while tropical plants may prefer more consistent moisture. Understand the specific needs of each plant in your collection.

7. Seasonal Adjustments:

Adjust your watering routine seasonally. Plants may need more water during warmer months when they are actively growing, and less during winter when growth slows down. Be mindful of changes in humidity and temperature.

8. Morning Watering:

Water plants in the morning when possible. This allows excess moisture on leaves to evaporate during the day, reducing the risk of fungal issues. It also ensures that plants are hydrated when they enter their active daytime phase.

9. Use a Watering Can with a Fine Spout:

Choose a watering can with a fine spout to deliver water directly to the base of the plant. This helps avoid splashing water on leaves and keeps the watering process controlled.

10. Adjust Based on Plant Size:

Adjust your watering routine based on the size of the plant and its pot. Larger plants in larger pots generally require more water, while smaller plants may need less frequent watering.

11. Wilting as an Indicator:

While not all plants exhibit wilting as a sign of needing water, it can be an indicator for some. Learn the specific signs of dehydration for each plant in your collection.

12. Empty Saucers:

Empty saucers beneath pots to prevent stagnant water. Standing water in saucers can lead to root rot and attract pests. Discard any excess water that accumulates after watering.

By following these watering basics and tailoring your approach to the specific needs of your indoor plants, you can create a healthy and thriving environment for your green companions. Regular observation and adjustments will help you develop a watering routine that ensures optimal plant well-being.

Signs of Overwatering and Underwatering

Recognizing signs of overwatering and underwatering is crucial for maintaining the health of your indoor plants.

Signs of Overwatering:

1. Wilting:

While it may seem counterintuitive, overwatering can lead to wilting. This is because excessive moisture in the soil can suffocate the roots, hindering their ability to absorb water.

2. Yellowing Leaves:

Yellowing leaves, especially if the yellowing starts at the base of the plant and progresses upwards, can be a sign of overwatering. This often indicates root rot caused by waterlogged soil.

3. Root Rot:

If you notice a foul smell emanating from the soil and the roots appear mushy or discolored, it could be a sign of root rot, a common issue resulting from overwatering.

4. Mold or Fungus Growth:

Excessive moisture can create a favorable environment for mold or fungus to grow on the soil surface. If you see white, fuzzy patches or mold growth, it may indicate overwatering.

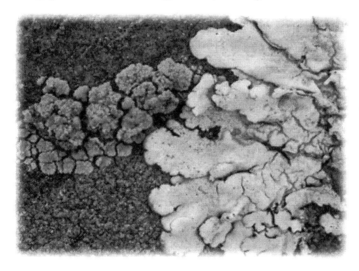

5. Leaf Drop:

Overwatered plants may drop leaves as a response to stress. This is particularly common in indoor plants that are sensitive to waterlogged conditions.

6. Soft or Mushy Stems:

Stems that feel soft or mushy to the touch can be a sign of overwatering, as the excessive moisture affects the plant's structural integrity.

7. Edema:

Edema occurs when plant cells absorb more water than they can release, resulting in blister-like growths on the undersides of leaves. This condition is often associated with overwatering.

Signs of Underwatering:

1. Wilting:

Wilting is a clear sign of underwatering. Insufficient water supply causes cells to lose turgor pressure, leading to wilting leaves.

2. Dry or Crispy Leaves:

Leaves that feel dry or crispy to the touch can indicate a lack of water. This is often accompanied by a change in leaf color, with the edges becoming brown.

3. Yellowing Leaves:

While yellowing can also be a sign of overwatering, in some cases, underwatered plants exhibit yellowing, starting from the tips and progressing towards the center of the leaf.

4. Curled or Shriveled Leaves:

Lack of water can cause leaves to curl or shrivel. This is the plant's way of conserving water by reducing surface area exposed to the air.

5. Stunted Growth:

Insufficient water can lead to stunted growth as the plant struggles to carry out essential processes like photosynthesis.

6. Leaf Drop:

In severe cases of underwatering, plants may drop leaves to conserve water. This is a survival mechanism to reduce water loss through transpiration.

7. Slow Recovery After Watering:

Underwatered plants may recover slowly after watering. If the soil is extremely dry, it may take some time for the roots to absorb and distribute water to the rest of the plant.

Observing these signs and adjusting your watering routine accordingly is key to maintaining a balance and ensuring the well-being of your indoor plants. Regularly assess the soil moisture, consider the specific needs of each plant, and make adjustments based on the environmental conditions in your home.

Fertilizing Your Indoor Garden

Fertilizing your indoor garden is essential for providing plants with the nutrients they need for healthy growth.

1. Choose the Right Fertilizer:

Select a balanced, water-soluble fertilizer designed for indoor plants. Different formulations cater to specific needs, such as promoting flowering or supporting foliage growth. Choose a fertilizer with a nutrient ratio suitable for your plants.

2. Follow the Recommended Schedule:

Adhere to the recommended fertilizing schedule provided on the fertilizer packaging or follow general guidelines for the specific types of plants you are growing. Over-fertilizing can lead to nutrient imbalances and harm plant health.

3. Dilute Fertilizer Properly:

Dilute the fertilizer according to the instructions. Using a concentration higher than recommended can lead to fertilizer burn, causing damage to the roots and leaves of your plants.

4. Apply Fertilizer to Moist Soil:

Apply fertilizer to moist soil to prevent potential root damage. Water the soil before applying the fertilizer, as this allows for better nutrient absorption by the roots.

5. Fertilize During the Growing Season:

Fertilize your plants during their active growing season, typically in spring and summer. Reduce or eliminate fertilizer applications during the dormant or slower growth periods in fall and winter.

6. Consider Plant-Specific Needs:

Some plants have specific nutrient requirements. Research the specific needs of the plants in your indoor garden and choose a fertilizer that aligns with those requirements.

7. Alternate Between Watering and Fertilizing:

Alternate between regular waterings and fertilizing sessions. This helps prevent salt buildup in the soil, a common issue associated with continuous fertilization.

8. Use Organic Fertilizers:

Consider using organic fertilizers for a natural and slow-release nutrient supply. Organic options contribute to soil health and microbial activity.

9. Be Mindful of Microelements:

Ensure that the fertilizer you choose contains essential microelements like iron, manganese, and zinc. These micronutrients are crucial for overall plant health.

10. Adjust Fertilizer Amounts for Container Size:

Adjust the amount of fertilizer based on the size of the plant container. Larger pots may require more fertilizer to supply nutrients to a greater volume of soil.

11. Flush Soil Periodically:

Periodically flush the soil with plain water to remove excess salts that may accumulate from fertilizing. This helps prevent salt buildup, which can damage plant roots.

12. Monitor Plant Response:

Pay attention to how your plants respond to fertilization. If you observe signs of nutrient deficiency or excess (such as yellowing leaves or leaf burn), adjust your fertilizing routine accordingly.

Remember that individual plants may have different fertilizing needs, so tailor your approach based on the specific requirements of each species. Regular observation, appropriate adjustments, and a balanced fertilizing regimen contribute to the overall health and vibrancy of your indoor garden.

Organic and Synthetic Fertilizers

Organic and synthetic fertilizers are two main types of fertilizers used in gardening, each with its own set of advantages and considerations.

Organic Fertilizers:

1. Derived from Natural Sources:

Organic fertilizers are derived from natural sources such as plant and animal materials. Common examples include compost, manure, bone meal, and fish emulsion.

2. Slow-Release Nutrients:

Organic fertilizers generally release nutrients slowly over time. They rely on microbial activity in the soil to break down the organic matter and make nutrients available to plants.

3. Improves Soil Structure:

Organic fertilizers contribute to the improvement of soil structure and fertility. They enhance the soil's water retention, aeration, and nutrient-holding capacity.

4. Sustainable and Environmentally Friendly:

Organic fertilizers are considered more environmentally friendly and sustainable. They often involve recycling organic waste materials and promote soil health and biodiversity.

5. Reduced Risk of Over-Fertilization:

Organic fertilizers are less likely to cause over-fertilization, as the nutrients are released gradually. This can be beneficial for plants that require a steady nutrient supply.

6. Builds Soil Microbial Activity:

Organic fertilizers support and enhance the activity of beneficial microorganisms in the soil, fostering a healthier soil ecosystem.

7. Long-Term Soil Enrichment:

Regular use of organic fertilizers contributes to long-term soil enrichment, making them suitable for sustainable and organic gardening practices.

Synthetic Fertilizers:

1. Chemically Manufactured:

Synthetic fertilizers are chemically manufactured and formulated to provide specific nutrient concentrations. They are often composed of salts or compounds containing nitrogen, phosphorus, and potassium.

2. Immediate Nutrient Availability:

Synthetic fertilizers provide immediate nutrient availability to plants. The nutrients are usually in a form that plants can readily absorb, promoting quick growth and development.

3. Precise Nutrient Control:

Synthetic fertilizers offer precise control over nutrient ratios. This allows gardeners to tailor fertilization to the specific needs of different plants, promoting optimal growth.

4. Convenient and Readily Available:

Synthetic fertilizers are widely available and convenient to use. They come in various formulations, including liquid, granular, and slow-release pellets, providing flexibility in application.

5. Address Specific Nutrient Deficiencies:

Synthetic fertilizers are effective in quickly addressing specific nutrient deficiencies in plants. Gardeners can apply targeted formulations based on observed symptoms.

6. Less Bulky and Easier to Store:

Synthetic fertilizers are often less bulky than organic alternatives and easier to store. They have a longer shelf life and are more concentrated, requiring less storage space.

7. Potential Environmental Concerns:

Overuse of synthetic fertilizers can contribute to environmental concerns, such as nutrient runoff into water bodies, leading to issues like algal blooms and water pollution.

8. May Disrupt Soil Microbial Balance:

Continuous use of synthetic fertilizers without organic amendments can potentially disrupt the natural balance of soil microorganisms, affecting long-term soil health.

Choosing between organic and synthetic fertilizers depends on individual preferences, gardening practices, and environmental considerations. Some gardeners prefer a combination of both for a balanced approach that addresses specific plant needs while promoting overall soil health.

Troubleshooting Common Nutrient Issues

Troubleshooting common nutrient issues in indoor plants involves identifying specific symptoms and addressing the underlying causes.

1. Yellowing Leaves:

Possible Cause: Nitrogen deficiency.

Solution: Apply a balanced fertilizer with higher nitrogen content. Ensure that the fertilizer is suitable for the specific plants you are growing.

2. Browning Leaf Edges:

Possible Cause: Potassium deficiency.

Solution: Use a fertilizer with a higher potassium content. Check for proper drainage, as poor drainage can affect potassium uptake.

3. General Leaf Yellowing:

Possible Cause: Iron deficiency.

Solution: Apply a fertilizer containing chelated iron. Adjust the pH of the soil if it's too high, as alkaline soils can impede iron absorption.

4. Purple or Reddish Leaves:

Possible Cause: Phosphorus deficiency.

Solution: Use a fertilizer with higher phosphorus content. Ensure that the pH of the soil is within the appropriate range for phosphorus absorption.

5. Stunted Growth and Small Leaves:

Possible Cause: Overall nutrient deficiency, especially nitrogen.

Solution: Apply a balanced, complete fertilizer to address multiple nutrient deficiencies. Follow the recommended application rates.

6. Leaf Burn or Tip Burn:

Possible Cause: Excessive fertilizer concentration.

Solution: Dilute the fertilizer according to the recommended rates. Water the plants thoroughly to flush excess salts from the soil.

7. Leaf Curling:

Possible Cause: Magnesium deficiency.

Solution: Apply a fertilizer with magnesium or use Epsom salts. Check the pH level, as magnesium availability is influenced by pH.

8. Leaf Drop:

Possible Cause: Over-fertilization, root damage, or environmental stress.

Solution: Review your fertilizing routine, ensure proper watering practices, and address any environmental factors stressing the plants.

9. Irregular Leaf Coloration:

Possible Cause: Micronutrient deficiencies (e.g., iron, manganese, zinc).

Solution: Apply a micronutrient-rich fertilizer or foliar spray. Adjust the pH if necessary, as it influences micronutrient availability.

10. Wilting Despite Adequate Watering:

Possible Cause: Root damage due to excessive salt accumulation.

Solution: Flush the soil thoroughly with water to remove excess salts. Adjust your watering and fertilizing practices to prevent salt buildup.

11. Leaf Spots:

Possible Cause: Nutrient imbalances, fungal or bacterial infections.

Solution: Correct nutrient deficiencies or excesses. Treat fungal or bacterial issues with appropriate fungicides or bactericides.

12. Slowed Growth:

Possible Cause: Inadequate nutrients for the growth phase.

Solution: Apply a fertilizer with a higher nitrogen ratio to support vegetative growth. Ensure proper overall care, including light, water, and temperature.

Regularly monitor your plants for signs of nutrient issues and adjust your fertilizing routine accordingly. Conduct soil tests if needed to identify specific nutrient deficiencies or imbalances, and choose fertilizers that address the specific needs of your indoor plants.

GARDEN PLANNER

GARDEN PLANNER

Common Name:	Botanical Name:
Crop Variety:	Date Planted:
Date Harvested:	Date Transplanted:

☐ Flower ☐ Fruit ☐ Herb ☐ Vegetable ☐ Tree

☐ Annual ☐ Edible ☐ Medicinal

☐ Perennial ☐ Spices ☐ Repellent

☐ Biennial ☐ Tea ☐ Natural Dyes

Purchased Information:	Watering Schedule:
Vendor:	
Cost:	Sunlight Exposure:
Quantity Purchased:	

Care Instructions:	Disease/Insects Problems:
	Treatments and Results:
Fertilizers to Use:	Additional Notes:

GARDEN PLANNER

GARDEN PLANNER

Common Name:	Botanical Name:
Crop Variety:	Date Planted:
Date Harvested:	Date Transplanted:

☐ Flower   ☐ Fruit   ☐ Herb   ☐ Vegetable   ☐ Tree

☐ Annual	☐ Edible	☐ Medicinal
☐ Perennial	☐ Spices	☐ Repellent
☐ Biennial	☐ Tea	☐ Natural Dyes

Purchased Information:	Watering Schedule:
Vendor:	
Cost:	Sunlight Exposure:
Quantity Purchased:	

Care Instructions:	Disease/Insects Problems:
	Treatments and Results:
Fertilizers to Use:	Additional Notes:

CHAPTER FOUR:

MAINTAINING A HEALTHY INDOOR GARDEN

Pruning and Trimming Techniques

Pruning and trimming are essential techniques for maintaining the health, shape, and appearance of indoor plants. Here's a guide on the basic techniques and considerations for effective pruning and trimming:

1. Tools:

- Use sharp, clean pruning shears or scissors appropriate for the size of the plant.
- Disinfect tools with rubbing alcohol before and after each use to prevent the spread of diseases.

2. **Reasons for Pruning:**

- **Remove Dead or Yellowing Leaves:** Trim away dead or yellowing leaves to improve the overall appearance of the plant and encourage new growth.

- **Control Size and Shape:** Prune to control the size and shape of the plant, promoting a more compact and aesthetically pleasing form.

- **Encourage Bushier Growth:** Pinch or prune the tips of branches to encourage lateral growth and create a fuller, bushier plant.

- **Remove Diseased or Damaged Parts:** Trim away any diseased or damaged parts of the plant to prevent the spread of infections and promote overall plant health.

3. **Basic Pruning Techniques:**

- **Pinching:** Use your fingers to pinch off the tips of stems to encourage branching and a more compact growth habit.

- **Thinning:** Remove entire stems or branches at the base to improve air circulation and reduce plant density.

- **Heading Back:** Cut back the main stems or branches to promote branching and denser growth.

4. **When to Prune:**

- **Regular Maintenance:** Perform light pruning regularly to maintain the shape and health of the plant.
- **After Flowering:** For flowering plants, prune immediately after the flowering period to encourage new growth.
- **During Growth Periods:** Prune during the active growing season for optimal recovery and regrowth.

5. **Specific Plant Considerations:**

- **Foliage Plants:** Prune to maintain a balanced shape and remove leggy growth. Pinch or trim back regularly to promote bushier growth.
- **Flowering Plants:** Trim spent flowers to encourage continuous blooming. Prune after flowering to shape the plant and remove dead or diseased parts.
- **Vining Plants:** Prune to control the length and encourage lateral growth. Support vining plants with stakes or trellises.
- **Succulents:** Remove dead or damaged leaves, and prune to shape and control size. Be cautious with over-pruning as succulents store water in their leaves.

6. **Tips for Successful Pruning:**

- **Start Small:** Begin with light pruning, especially if you are unsure about the plant's response. You can always prune more if needed.

- **Observe Plant Response:** Monitor how the plant responds to pruning. Healthy new growth is a positive sign.
- **Sterilize Tools:** Disinfect pruning tools between plants to prevent the spread of diseases.
- **Consider Seasonal Changes:** Adjust pruning frequency and intensity based on seasonal changes in growth patterns.

Remember that different plants may require specific pruning techniques, so it's essential to understand the characteristics of the particular plants in your indoor garden. Regular, thoughtful pruning contributes to the overall well-being and appearance of your indoor plants.

Pest Control Strategies

Effective pest control is crucial for maintaining the health and vitality of indoor plants. Here are some strategies to help you manage and prevent pests in your indoor garden:

1. **Regular Inspection:**

Routine Checks: Regularly inspect your plants for signs of pests, such as discolored leaves, holes, or visible insects. Early detection allows for prompt intervention.

2. **Isolation:**

Quarantine New Plants: Place newly acquired plants in isolation for a few weeks to monitor for any signs of pests before introducing them to your main collection.

3. Natural Predators:

Beneficial Insects: Introduce natural predators such as ladybugs or predatory mites, which can help control common pests like aphids or spider mites.

4. Neem Oil:

Neem Oil Spray: Neem oil is an effective and organic solution for controlling various pests. Mix with water and a few drops of dish soap to create a neem oil spray. Apply it to both sides of leaves.

5. Insecticidal Soap:

Homemade or Store-Bought: Insecticidal soap is an effective remedy for soft-bodied pests like aphids and spider mites. You can make your own or purchase a commercial option.

6. Diatomaceous Earth:

Natural Pest Control: Diatomaceous earth is a powder that consists of fossilized diatoms. Sprinkle it around the base of plants to create a barrier that can deter crawling insects.

7. Sticky Traps:

Yellow or Blue Traps: Use sticky traps to catch flying insects. Yellow or blue traps are especially effective against fungus gnats, whiteflies, and other flying pests.

8. Horticultural Oils:

Summer and Dormant Oils: Horticultural oils are effective against scale insects, mites, and certain other pests. Summer oils are used during the growing season, while dormant oils are applied in winter.

9. Physical Removal:

Handpicking: For larger pests like caterpillars or beetles, manually remove them from the plants. Wearing gloves can help protect your hands.

10. Humidity Management:

Adequate Humidity: Maintain proper humidity levels to discourage pests like spider mites, which thrive in dry conditions. Regularly misting plants can help deter mites.

11. Cultural Practices:

Proper Watering: Avoid overwatering, as standing water can attract pests like fungus gnats. Ensure good drainage to prevent waterlogged soil.

12. Pruning Infested Areas:

Remove Infested Parts: Prune and discard heavily infested parts of the plant to prevent the spread of pests to healthy areas.

13. Soil Sterilization:

Prevent Soil Pests: Sterilize soil before using it for new plants to reduce the risk of soil-borne pests. Baking soil in the oven or using a microwave are common methods.

14. Chemical Treatments (As a Last Resort):

Commercial Insecticides: If pests persist, consider using commercial insecticides as a last resort. Follow instructions carefully and choose products safe for indoor use.

15. Educate Yourself:

Identify Pests: Learn to identify common pests and their life cycles. Knowing your enemy is essential for effective pest management.

Combining these strategies and adapting them to the specific needs of your indoor plants will help you create a healthy environment with minimal pest-related issues. Regular vigilance and proactive measures are key to successful pest control.

Disease Prevention and Management

Preventing and managing diseases is crucial for maintaining the health of your indoor plants. Here's a guide to help you establish effective disease prevention and management strategies:

1. Quarantine New Plants:

Isolate New Additions: Place new plants in quarantine for a few weeks before introducing them to your main collection. This helps prevent the spread of potential diseases.

2. Healthy Plant Practices:

Proper Care: Maintain overall plant health through proper watering, appropriate lighting, and adequate ventilation. Healthy plants are more resistant to diseases.

3. Air Circulation:

Good Ventilation: Ensure proper air circulation around your plants. Use fans to promote air movement, which helps prevent conditions favorable to fungal diseases.

4. Water Management:

Avoid Overwatering: Overwatering can lead to root rot and other fungal issues. Allow the soil to dry out slightly between waterings to prevent waterlogged conditions.

5. Sterilize Tools:

Clean Pruning Tools: Disinfect pruning tools with rubbing alcohol before and after use. This helps prevent the transmission of diseases between plants.

6. Proper Spacing:

Adequate Plant Spacing: Ensure proper spacing between plants to minimize the risk of diseases spreading. Crowded plants can create conditions conducive to fungal growth.

7. Remove Infected Plant Material:

Prune Affected Parts: Promptly prune and remove any parts of the plant that show signs of disease. Dispose of the infected material away from other plants.

8. Copper-Based Fungicides:

Preventative Treatment: Apply copper-based fungicides preventatively to protect plants from common fungal diseases. Follow product instructions carefully.

9. Neem Oil:

Antifungal Properties: Neem oil, in addition to its insecticidal properties, also has antifungal properties. Use neem oil as a preventive measure against fungal diseases.

10.   Fungus Gnat Prevention:

Avoid Overwatering: Fungus gnats thrive in moist conditions. Keep the topsoil dry between waterings to deter these pests and prevent associated diseases.

11. Humidity Management:

Control Humidity Levels: Maintain appropriate humidity levels. Lower humidity can help prevent the development of fungal diseases, especially powdery mildew.

12. Use Disease-Resistant Varieties:

Select Resistant Plants: When possible, choose plant varieties that are known to be resistant to common diseases prevalent in indoor gardening.

13. Beneficial Microorganisms:

Inoculate Soil: Introduce beneficial microorganisms, such as mycorrhizal fungi, to the soil. These organisms form symbiotic relationships with plant roots and can enhance disease resistance.

14. Avoid Cross-Contamination:

Sanitize Hands and Tools: Wash your hands and sterilize tools after handling infected plants to avoid cross-contamination.

15. Monitor for Early Signs:

Regular Inspections: Conduct regular inspections for early signs of diseases. Early detection allows for prompt intervention and management.

16. Quarantine Affected Plants:

Isolate Infected Plants: If a plant shows signs of disease, isolate it from healthy plants to prevent the spread of the pathogen.

17. Chemical Treatments (As a Last Resort):

Fungicides or Bactericides: If diseases persist, consider using fungicides or bactericides as a last resort. Choose products suitable for indoor use and follow recommended application rates.

By incorporating these disease prevention and management strategies, you can create a resilient indoor garden that is less susceptible to common diseases. Regular observation, timely intervention, and maintaining a healthy environment are essential components of successful disease control.

Monitoring Plant Growth and Health

Monitoring plant growth and health is essential for ensuring the success of your indoor garden.

1. Regular Visual Inspection:

Observation Routine: Set a regular schedule for visually inspecting your plants. Check for any changes in color, leaf texture, and overall appearance. Early detection of issues is crucial.

2. Record Keeping:

Plant Journal: Keep a plant journal or log where you record observations, watering schedules, fertilization details, and any changes you make. This helps identify patterns and track plant development.

3. Height and Spread Measurements:

Growth Metrics: Measure the height and spread of your plants regularly. Documenting changes in size provides insights into the growth rate and overall health of the plant.

4. Leaf Examination:

Leaf Color: Monitor the color of leaves. Changes in color can indicate nutrient deficiencies, pests, or diseases. Yellowing, browning, or spotting may require attention.

5. Assess Soil Moisture:

Finger Test: Regularly check soil moisture by inserting your finger into the top inch of the soil. Adjust your watering routine based on the specific needs of each plant.

6. Inspect for Pests:

Underside of Leaves: Examine the undersides of leaves for pests, such as spider mites or aphids. Look for webbing, discoloration, or small insects that may indicate an infestation.

7. Monitor Growth Patterns:

Directional Growth: Observe the direction of growth. If a plant is leaning excessively toward the light source, it may need repositioning to maintain a balanced form.

8. Assess Root Health:

Root Zone Inspection: If possible, assess the roots when repotting or during routine maintenance. Healthy roots are firm and white, while rotting roots may appear brown and mushy.

9. Flower and Fruit Development:

Flowering Patterns: Monitor the development of flowers and fruits. Ensure that flowering plants receive adequate light and nutrients to support these processes.

10.   Consider Seasonal Changes:

Seasonal Adjustments: Be aware of seasonal variations in growth. Some plants may go through periods of dormancy or reduced growth during certain seasons.

11. Temperature and Humidity Impact:

Environmental   Conditions: Understand   how temperature and humidity affect your plants. Adjust environmental conditions if needed, especially for temperature-sensitive species.

12. Leaf and Stem Health:

Inspect for Diseases: Regularly check for signs of diseases, such as spots, discoloration, or wilting. Promptly address any disease issues to prevent further spread.

13. Overall Plant Structure:

Vigorous Growth: Assess the overall structure of the plant. Vigorous growth with a well-balanced form is an indicator of good health.

14. Evaluate Response to Care:

Adapt Your Care Routine: If you notice changes in your plants, adapt your care routine accordingly. This may involve adjusting light exposure, watering frequency, or fertilization.

15. Use Technology:

Plant Apps or Sensors: Consider using plant monitoring apps or sensors that measure environmental conditions and provide insights into your plant's health.

By consistently monitoring your indoor plants using these strategies, you can detect issues early, make informed adjustments to your care routine, and foster a thriving and healthy indoor garden. Regular attention and proactive measures contribute to the overall well-being of your plants.

Seasonal Adjustments for Indoor Plants

Adapting your care routine to the changing seasons is essential for maintaining the health and well-being of indoor plants. Here are seasonal adjustments you can make for your indoor garden:

1. **Spring:**

- **Increased Growth:** Spring is a period of increased growth for many plants. Adjust your fertilization routine to support this growth, providing a balanced fertilizer with slightly higher nitrogen content.

- **Consider Repotting:** If your plants have outgrown their containers, spring is an ideal time for repotting. Refresh the soil, inspect roots, and provide room for new growth.

- **Gradual Transition to Outdoor Sunlight:** If you plan to move any indoor plants outdoors for the summer, gradually acclimate them to increased sunlight to avoid sunburn.

2. **Summer:**

- **Optimal Watering:** With warmer temperatures, plants may require more frequent watering. Adjust your watering routine based on the specific needs of each plant and the environmental conditions.

- **Increased Humidity:** Maintain adequate humidity levels, especially if you're using air conditioning, which can reduce indoor humidity. Misting or using a humidifier can help.
- **Monitor for Pests:** Increased temperatures can attract pests. Regularly inspect your plants for signs of infestations and take preventive measures.

3. **Fall:**
- **Reduced Growth:** As daylight hours decrease, many plants experience a slowdown in growth. Adjust fertilization to reflect the decreased need for nutrients.
- **Prepare for Lower Light Levels:** With the approach of winter, be prepared for lower light levels. Move light-sensitive plants to brighter locations or supplement with artificial light.
- **Scale Back Watering:** As plants enter dormancy or experience reduced growth, scale back on watering frequency. Allow the soil to dry out slightly between waterings.

4. **Winter:**
- **Decreased Watering:** Indoor plants generally require less water during winter. Be cautious not to overwater, as reduced light levels and lower temperatures slow down plant metabolism.

- **Watch for Drafts:** Cold drafts from windows or doors can stress plants. Keep them away from drafty areas, and provide additional insulation if necessary.
- **Limit Fertilization:** During winter, plants are often in a period of dormancy or reduced growth. Limit fertilization, providing only if there's active growth or signs of nutrient deficiency.
- **Maintain Consistent Temperatures:** Avoid extreme temperature fluctuations. Sudden drops in temperature can shock plants, while consistent temperatures help them acclimate.

5. **Year-Round Considerations:**

- **Rotate Plants:** Regularly rotate your plants to ensure even exposure to light. This helps prevent lopsided growth and encourages an even, well-balanced form.
- **Clean Leaves:** Keep plant leaves clean by gently wiping them with a damp cloth. Dust and debris can hinder light absorption and reduce overall plant health.
- **Monitor and Adjust Lighting:** If using artificial lighting, regularly check and adjust the positioning and intensity of lights based on plant needs and changing natural light conditions.

6. **Consistent Care:**

- **Observation is Key:** Regardless of the season, consistent observation is crucial. Pay attention to your plants' responses to environmental changes, adjusting care routines accordingly.

- **Adapt to Individual Plant Needs:** Each plant may have unique requirements. Be attentive to individual needs and adjust watering, light exposure, and care practices accordingly.

By making these seasonal adjustments, you can create an environment that supports the natural growth cycles of your indoor plants and ensures their well-being throughout the year.

CHAPTER FIVE:

EXPANDING YOUR INDOOR GARDEN

Propagation Methods for Indoor Plants

Propagating indoor plants is a rewarding way to expand your collection or share plants with friends. Here are common propagation methods for indoor plants:

1. Seed Propagation:

Collecting Seeds: Harvest seeds from mature plants and sow them in a suitable seed-starting mix. Follow specific requirements for each plant species regarding depth, light, and moisture.

2. Cutting Propagation:

Stem Cuttings: Snip a healthy stem from the parent plant, typically 4-6 inches in length, with at least one leaf node. Remove lower leaves and place the cutting in a rooting medium until roots develop.

Leaf Cuttings: Take a healthy leaf and cut it into sections, ensuring each segment has a vein. Plant these sections in a rooting medium to encourage root growth.

3. Division:

Root Division: Divide mature plants with multiple stems or crowns into smaller sections. Gently separate the roots and replant each division in its own container.

4. Offsets or Pups:

Separate Offsets: Some plants, like spider plants or aloe vera, produce offsets or pups. These small shoots can be gently separated from the parent plant and potted individually.

5. Layering:

Air Layering: Encourage roots to form on a portion of a stem while still attached to the parent plant. Once roots develop, cut the rooted section and plant it separately.

6. Bulb Offsets:

Separate Bulbs: Plants that grow from bulbs, like certain types of lilies, produce offsets. Separate these bulbs and plant them to propagate new plants.

7. Runners:

Runners or Stolons: Some plants produce runners or stolons with new plantlets. Once the plantlets have roots, detach them from the runner and pot them.

8. Grafting:

Grafting: Joining two plant parts to create a single plant. This is often used for combining desirable traits or creating stronger rootstocks.

9. Tissue Culture:

Micropropagation: Advanced technique involving growing plant cells in a controlled environment to produce identical copies of the parent plant.

10.   Water Propagation:

Rooting in Water: Some plants can be propagated by placing cuttings in water until roots develop. Once roots are established, transplant the cutting into soil.

11. Offsets or Bulblets:

Harvest Bulblets: Certain plants, like garlic or certain lilies, produce bulblets. Harvest these smaller bulbs and plant them to grow new plants.

12. Rhizome Division:

Divide Rhizomes: For plants with rhizomes (underground stems), divide them into sections and replant. Examples include bearded irises and certain ferns.

13. Leaf Vein Propagation:

Leaf Vein Cuttings: Some plants can be propagated by cutting along the veins of a leaf and placing the sections in a rooting medium until roots develop.

14. Sucker Propagation:

Harvest Suckers: Some plants produce suckers, shoots that emerge from the base of the plant. Harvest these and transplant them to grow new plants.

Choose the propagation method that suits the type of plant you are working with, and consider the specific requirements of each species. Experimenting with different methods can be a fun and educational way to expand your indoor garden.

Introducing Different Plant Varieties

Introducing a variety of plant species to your indoor garden can enhance its beauty and diversity.

1. Consider Light Requirements:

Group Plants with Similar Light Needs: Arrange plants with similar light requirements together to ensure they thrive. Some plants prefer bright, indirect light, while others thrive in lower light conditions.

2. Select a Mix of Sizes:

Create Visual Interest: Mix small, medium, and large plants to create visual interest. Tall or trailing plants can be placed near shorter ones to add dimension to your indoor garden.

3. Vary Leaf Shapes and Colors:

Diversity in Foliage: Choose plants with different leaf shapes, sizes, and colors. This diversity adds aesthetic appeal to your indoor space.

4. Mix Flowering and Foliage Plants:

Balance with Blooms: Incorporate flowering plants among foliage varieties to introduce pops of color. Consider the blooming seasons of different plants for continuous floral interest.

5. Include Different Plant Forms:

Combine Upright and Trailing Forms: Combine plants with upright growth habits and trailing forms. This creates a dynamic and visually pleasing arrangement.

6. Explore Various Textures:

Texture Variety: Select plants with various textures—smooth, fuzzy, glossy, or variegated leaves. Texture diversity adds tactile interest to your indoor garden.

7. Incorporate Edible Plants:

Herbs or Edibles: Introduce edible plants like herbs to your indoor garden. Not only do they provide fresh ingredients for cooking, but they also add a pleasant aroma.

8. Experiment with Different Plant Families:

Explore Plant Families: Choose plants from different botanical families to experience a wide range of growth habits and characteristics. This can also diversify care requirements.

9. Add Air-Purifying Plants:

Enhance Air Quality: Include air-purifying plants, such as snake plants, spider plants, or peace lilies, to improve indoor air quality.

10.   Introduce Unusual or Unique Species:

Uncommon Varieties: Consider adding unusual or unique plant varieties to spark conversation and make your indoor garden stand out.

11. Account for Growth Rates:

Balance Growth Rates: Be mindful of the growth rates of different plants. Some may require more frequent pruning or repotting than others.

12. Consider Watering and Maintenance Needs:

Compatible Care Needs: Group plants with similar watering and maintenance needs. This simplifies care routines and ensures each plant receives appropriate attention.

13. Create Theme-Based Arrangements:

Themed Displays: Arrange plants based on a theme, such as tropical, desert, or succulent gardens. Themed arrangements provide a cohesive and visually appealing display.

14. Rotate Seasonal Plants:

Seasonal Rotation: Introduce seasonal plants to celebrate different times of the year. Swap out certain plants to accommodate seasonal changes in light and temperature.

15. Personalize with Favorites:

Include Personal Favorites: Include plants that resonate with you personally or have sentimental value. Your indoor garden should reflect your preferences and style.

By incorporating a variety of plant species with thoughtful consideration for their needs and aesthetics, you can create a diverse and vibrant indoor garden that brings joy and beauty to your living space.

Creating Attractive Indoor Garden Designs

Designing an attractive indoor garden involves combining different plants, containers, and decorative elements to create a visually pleasing and harmonious space. Here are tips to help you create an appealing indoor garden design:

1. **Choose a Design Theme:**

Consistent Theme: Establish a theme for your indoor garden, whether it's tropical, minimalist, or eclectic. A consistent theme helps create a cohesive and visually appealing design.

2. **Consider Plant Combinations:**

Contrast and Balance: Combine plants with contrasting leaf shapes, sizes, and colors to add visual interest. Balance the arrangement by distributing plants of varying heights and forms.

3. **Use Stylish Containers:**

Aesthetic Planters: Select decorative containers that complement your interior style. Consider various materials, such as ceramic, metal, or woven baskets, to add texture and personality.

4. Create Focal Points:

Highlight Key Plants: Designate focal points with standout plants or larger specimens. Place them strategically to draw attention and create a focal area within the indoor garden.

5. Consider Vertical Gardens:

Wall-Mounted Displays: Utilize vertical space by creating wall-mounted plant displays or installing shelves for a cascading effect. This maximizes space and adds a dynamic visual element.

6. Incorporate Decorative Elements:

Art, Sculptures, or Decor: Enhance your indoor garden with decorative elements like artwork, sculptures, or decorative stones. These elements can complement your plant arrangement and contribute to the overall design.

7. Play with Color Palettes:

Harmonious Color Scheme: Choose a harmonious color palette for both plants and containers. Consider the existing colors in your interior space to create a cohesive look.

8. Create Pathways or Zones:

Organized Layout: Organize your indoor garden into distinct zones or pathways. This helps define spaces and adds structure to the design.

9. Experiment with Lighting:

Strategic Lighting: Integrate strategic lighting to highlight specific plants or create a cozy ambiance. Consider using decorative plant stands with built-in lighting for an elegant touch.

10.   Group Plants Thoughtfully:

Grouping by Height and Form: Arrange plants in groups based on their height and form. This creates a sense of order and balance within the indoor garden.

11. Seasonal Rotations:

Rotate Seasonal Plants: Introduce seasonal plants and rotate them throughout the year to keep the design fresh and aligned with changing seasons.

12. Incorporate Functional Elements:

Multipurpose Furniture: Use multipurpose furniture like plant stands, shelves, or tables to display plants while serving a practical function. This maximizes space and utility.

13. Consider Fragrance:

Fragrant Plants: Include fragrant plants, such as lavender or herbs, to add a sensory element to your indoor garden. Fragrance contributes to the overall ambiance.

14. Personalize with Sentimental Items:

Personal Touches: Infuse personal elements such as family heirlooms, vintage planters, or sentimental items that hold meaning. This adds a unique and personal touch to the design.

15. Adapt to Your Living Space:

Scale to Room Size: Consider the size of your room when selecting plants and containers. Scale the design appropriately to fit the available space and avoid overcrowding.

By incorporating these design principles, you can create an attractive and inviting indoor garden that not only enhances the aesthetics of your living space but also provides a tranquil and enjoyable environment.

Incorporating Edible Plants Indoors

Incorporating edible plants into your indoor garden is a rewarding way to enjoy fresh ingredients while adding a practical and decorative element to your space. Here's how to incorporate edible plants indoors:

1. **Choose Suitable Edibles:**

- **Herbs:** Herbs like basil, mint, rosemary, thyme, and parsley are popular choices for indoor gardening due to their compact size and versatility in cooking.

- **Salad Greens:** Varieties of lettuce, spinach, and microgreens can be grown indoors for fresh salads.
- **Fruit-bearing Plants:** Compact fruit-bearing plants like strawberries or dwarf citrus trees can be grown in larger containers.

2. **Select Appropriate Containers:**

- **Well-Draining Pots:** Choose containers with drainage holes to prevent waterlogged soil. Use containers that suit the size and growth habits of your chosen edible plants.
- **Windowsill Planters:** Utilize windowsill planters for smaller herbs. These can be placed on kitchen windowsills for easy access.

3. **Provide Adequate Light:**

- **Bright, Indirect Light:** Most edible plants thrive in bright, indirect light. Place them near a south or west-facing window where they can receive several hours of sunlight daily.
- **Supplemental Lighting:** If natural light is limited, consider using grow lights to provide additional light for optimal plant growth.

4. **Optimize Soil and Fertilization:**

- **Quality Potting Mix:** Use a well-draining potting mix enriched with organic matter for optimal plant growth.
- **Balanced Fertilizer:** Provide a balanced, water-soluble fertilizer designed for edible plants. Follow the recommended application rates to avoid over-fertilization.

5. **Watering and Humidity:**

- **Consistent Moisture:** Keep the soil consistently moist but not waterlogged. Water when the top inch of the soil feels dry.
- **Maintain Humidity:** Some edible plants, especially herbs, appreciate higher humidity levels. Mist the leaves or use a humidifier if needed.

6. **Consider Companion Planting:**

- **Companion Planting:** Arrange edible plants that complement each other in terms of growth habits and care needs. For example, grow herbs alongside vegetables that share similar water and light requirements.

7. **Rotate and Harvest Regularly:**

- **Encourage Bushier Growth:** Regularly rotate plants to ensure even exposure to light. Harvest herbs regularly to encourage bushier growth and prolong productivity.

8. Control Pests Naturally:

- **Natural Pest Management:** Use natural pest control methods like introducing beneficial insects, neem oil, or homemade insecticidal soap to manage pests without harmful chemicals.

9. Grow Vertical Gardens:

- **Vertical Planters:** Maximize space by growing edible plants in vertical planters or on wall-mounted shelves. This is especially useful for compact kitchens.

10.   Utilize Kitchen Space:

- **Kitchen Countertops:** Place small herb pots directly on kitchen countertops for easy access while cooking.

11. Experiment with Unusual Edibles:

- **Unique Varieties:** Explore less common edible plants or unique varieties that add interest to your indoor garden. Examples include edible flowers or uncommon herbs.

12. Maintain Good Air Circulation:

- **Proper Ventilation:** Ensure good air circulation around your indoor edible plants. This helps prevent issues like mold and supports overall plant health.

13. Harvest and Enjoy:

- **Regular Harvesting:** Harvest your edible plants regularly to enjoy fresh, flavorful ingredients in your meals.
- **Rotate Crops:** Consider rotating crops and introducing new varieties to keep your indoor garden diverse and interesting.

14. **Educate Yourself on Edible Plants:**
- **Understanding Growth Habits:** Learn about the specific needs and growth habits of each edible plant you incorporate. Understanding their requirements ensures successful cultivation.

15. **Adapt to Your Space:**
- **Scale to Available Space:** Tailor your indoor edible garden to the available space in your home. Optimize kitchen counters, windowsills, or designated garden areas.

By integrating edible plants into your indoor garden, you not only enhance your culinary experiences but also create a practical and aesthetically pleasing environment within your living space.

Troubleshooting Advanced Indoor Gardening Challenges

Troubleshooting advanced indoor gardening challenges requires a nuanced approach to address specific issues that may arise. Here are solutions to tackle some advanced challenges:

1. Nutrient Deficiencies:

Symptoms: Yellowing leaves, stunted growth, or leaf discoloration.

Solution: Conduct a soil test to identify nutrient deficiencies. Adjust fertilization based on test results, and consider using a balanced liquid fertilizer or micronutrient supplements.

2. Advanced Pest Infestations:

Symptoms: Severe leaf damage, visible pests, or widespread infestation.

Solution: Implement integrated pest management (IPM) strategies. Introduce beneficial insects, use neem oil or insecticidal soap, and isolate heavily infested plants. Regularly monitor and treat affected plants.

3. Root Rot:

Symptoms: Wilting, yellowing, or drooping leaves despite proper watering.

Solution: Improve soil drainage and avoid overwatering. Repot affected plants into fresh, well-draining soil. Consider using fungicides containing beneficial bacteria like Bacillus subtilis.

4. Lighting Issues:

Symptoms: Leggy growth, elongated stems, or yellowing leaves.

Solution: Assess the lighting conditions. Ensure plants receive the appropriate intensity and duration of light. Consider adjusting the placement of grow lights or increasing natural light exposure.

5. Temperature Extremes:

Symptoms: Leaf burn, wilting, or growth slowdown due to extreme temperatures.

Solution: Maintain consistent temperatures within the optimal range for your plants. Provide insulation against drafts, avoid placing plants near heaters or air conditioners, and use temperature-regulating devices if necessary.

6. Humidity Challenges:

Symptoms: Browning leaf edges, curling leaves, or increased susceptibility to pests.

Solution: Maintain optimal humidity levels for your plants. Use humidifiers, misting, or humidity trays to increase humidity. For lower humidity plants, group them together or use a dehumidifier.

7. Disease Outbreaks:

Symptoms: Spots, lesions, or unusual growth patterns on leaves.

Solution: Identify the specific disease and treat accordingly. Use fungicides or bactericides as recommended. Ensure good air circulation, proper sanitation, and quarantine affected plants.

8. Advanced Watering Challenges:

Symptoms: Overwatering leading to root rot or underwatering causing wilting and nutrient uptake issues.

Solution: Monitor soil moisture carefully. Adjust watering frequency based on plant needs and environmental conditions. Consider using self-watering containers or incorporating a moisture meter.

9. pH Imbalance:

Symptoms: Yellowing leaves, nutrient deficiencies, or poor growth despite adequate care.

Solution: Test the soil pH and adjust it to the appropriate range for your plants. Use pH-adjusting substances like dolomite lime for alkaline soils or sulfur for acidic soils.

10. Overcrowding and Plant Competition:

Symptoms: Reduced growth, competition for resources, and increased vulnerability to pests and diseases.

Solution: Space plants appropriately to prevent overcrowding. Consider repotting or dividing larger plants.

Adjust the layout to ensure each plant has sufficient access to light, water, and nutrients.

11. Advanced Pruning and Training:

Symptoms: Unruly growth, leggy stems, or uneven canopy.

Solution: Implement advanced pruning techniques, such as topping, pinching, or selective pruning, to shape plants. Utilize plant training methods like LST (Low Stress Training) or SCROG (Screen of Green) for controlled growth.

12. Soil Issues:

Symptoms: Compacted soil, poor drainage, or nutrient imbalances.

Solution: Amend soil with organic matter for improved structure and drainage. Conduct soil tests to identify and address nutrient imbalances. Consider repotting into fresh, well-aerated soil.

Addressing advanced indoor gardening challenges requires a comprehensive understanding of plant needs and potential issues. Regular monitoring, timely intervention, and a proactive approach to care are essential for maintaining a healthy and thriving indoor garden.

GARDEN PLANNER

GARDEN PLANNER

Common Name:	Botanical Name:
Crop Variety:	Date Planted:
Date Harvested:	Date Transplanted:

☐ Flower ☐ Fruit ☐ Herb ☐ Vegetable ☐ Tree

☐ Annual ☐ Edible ☐ Medicinal

☐ Perennial ☐ Spices ☐ Repellent

☐ Biennial ☐ Tea ☐ Natural Dyes

Purchased Information:	Watering Schedule:
Vendor:	
Cost:	Sunlight Exposure:
Quantity Purchased:	

Care Instructions:	Disease/Insects Problems:
	Treatments and Results:
Fertilizers to Use:	Additional Notes:

GARDEN PLANNER

GARDEN PLANNER

Common Name:	Botanical Name:
Crop Variety:	Date Planted:
Date Harvested:	Date Transplanted:

☐ Flower ☐ Fruit ☐ Herb ☐ Vegetable ☐ Tree

☐ Annual	☐ Edible	☐ Medicinal
☐ Perennial	☐ Spices	☐ Repellent
☐ Biennial	☐ Tea	☐ Natural Dyes

Purchased Information:	Watering Schedule:
Vendor:	
Cost:	Sunlight Exposure:
Quantity Purchased:	
Care Instructions:	Disease/Insects Problems:
	Treatments and Results:
Fertilizers to Use:	Additional Notes:

CONCLUSION

Venturing into the world of indoor gardening as a beginner offers a journey filled with discovery, growth, and the joy of cultivating a living oasis within the confines of your home.

This guide has aimed to equip beginners with the essential knowledge needed to embark on this fulfilling endeavor. From understanding the benefits of indoor gardening to selecting the right plants, creating an inviting space, and overcoming challenges, each chapter serves as a stepping stone toward becoming a confident and successful indoor gardener.

As you delve into the intricacies of nurturing your indoor garden, remember that patience and observation are key companions on this botanical journey. Tailoring your care routines to the unique needs of each plant, adapting to seasonal changes, and troubleshooting challenges will pave the way for a flourishing indoor oasis.

Indoor gardening is not merely a hobby; it's a therapeutic and transformative experience that connects individuals with nature in the comfort of their homes.

Whether you are cultivating edible herbs, vibrant flowers, or lush greenery, the rewards extend beyond aesthetics to include improved well-being and a sense of accomplishment. So, as you witness your indoor garden thrive and evolve, revel in the fulfillment of nurturing life within the confines of your own sanctuary. Happy gardening!

GARDEN PLANNER

GARDEN PLANNER

Common Name:	Botanical Name:
Crop Variety:	Date Planted:
Date Harvested:	Date Transplanted:

☐ Flower ☐ Fruit ☐ Herb ☐ Vegetable ☐ Tree

☐ Annual   ☐ Edible   ☐ Medicinal

☐ Perennial   ☐ Spices   ☐ Repellent

☐ Biennial   ☐ Tea   ☐ Natural Dyes

Purchased Information:	Watering Schedule:
Vendor:	
Cost:	Sunlight Exposure:
Quantity Purchased:	

Care Instructions:	Disease/Insects Problems:
	Treatments and Results:
Fertilizers to Use:	Additional Notes:

GARDEN PLANNER

Common Name:	Botanical Name:
Crop Variety:	Date Planted:
Date Harvested:	Date Transplanted:

☐ Flower ☐ Fruit ☐ Herb ☐ Vegetable ☐ Tree

☐ Annual	☐ Edible	☐ Medicinal
☐ Perennial	☐ Spices	☐ Repellent
☐ Biennial	☐ Tea	☐ Natural Dyes

Purchased Information:	Watering Schedule:
Vendor:	
Cost:	Sunlight Exposure:
Quantity Purchased:	
Care Instructions:	Disease/Insects Problems:
	Treatments and Results:
Fertilizers to Use:	Additional Notes:

Printed in Great Britain
by Amazon

2ada53f3-5657-4db0-bbd7-5dea4f309726R01